How to Build an Electronic Witness Well for Radionics (E-Well)

Mastering Radionics Series ™

by Peter V. Radatti

First Edition April 2017
Second Edition July 2020

SECOND EDITION

Those that purchased the first edition can get the free upgrade to the second edition at
www.radatti.com/books

How to Build an Electronic Witness Well for Radionics

Table of Contents

Table of Contents 2
Chapter 1 - Preface and Dedication 5
   Preface...5
   Preface Update 6
   Dedication 6
Chapter 2 – Copyright, ISBN and Legal Notices 7
   Copyright Notice and Editions...7
DISCLAIMER 8
Chapter 3 – How to Build an E-Well 10
Chapter 4 - How to use and suggested usage...21
    What results can you expect?...22
Chapter 5 - Rates used for the E-Well program..24
    Unlock-1 (Erase) – Gem Stones / Sand / Solids (no password) 24
    Lock-1 Gem Stones / Sand / Solids (no password)...24
    Hell Burner 1.0 (from Pete's library)...25
    ROSP Version 1.0 25
    VAMPIRE REPELLENT 26
   Start the process of spiritual healing:..27
   Prevent it from happening again:..27
   Reestablish proper and healthy connection to life-force:..28
   Soul Integration Repair Protocol 28
   Soul-to-Astral..29

- Soul-to-Astral Primary Information Circuit 29
- Soul-to-Astral Secondary Information Circuit 29
- Soul-to-Astral Third Information Circuit 30
- Soul-to-Astral Fourth Information Circuit 30
- Soul-to-Astral Fifth Information Circuit 30
- Soul-to-Astral Sixth Information Circuit 30
- Soul-to-Astral Seventh Information Circuit 31
- Soul-to-Astral Eighth Information Circuit (CRITICAL RATE) 31
- Soul-to-Astral Ninth Information Circuit 31
- Soul-to-Astral Tenth Information Circuit 31

Astral to Physical 32

- Astral To Physical Primary Information Circuit 32
- Astral To Physical Secondary Information Circuit 32
- Astral To Physical Third Information Circuit 32
- Astral To Physical Fourth Information Circuit 32
- Astral To Physical Fifth Information Circuit 33
- Astral To Physical Sixth Information Circuit 33
- Astral To Physical Seventh Information Circuit 33
- Astral To Physical Eighth Information Circuit 33
- Astral To Physical Ninth Information Circuit 34
- Astral To Physical Tenth Information Circuit 34

Soul-to-Astral-to-Physical Basic Structure 34

- Information that defines the basic structure of an Astral Body 35
- Information that defines the basic structure of a Physical Body 35
- Removal of Information that Does Not Belong in/on the Soul 35
- Removal of Information that damages the transfer of information from the Soul to the Astral Body 35
- Removal of Information that Does Not Belong in the Astral Body 36
- Removal of Information that damages the transfer of information from the Astral to the Physical Body. 36

Psychic Attack 37

Sacred Geometry Shapes and their Rates 39

Chapter 6 – New Material for Second Edition 40

- Isolate all witnesses so that no crosstalk or interaction of any kind is possible. ... 40
- Stove pipe all witnesses so that they are delivered to the radionics machine separately without any interaction with other witnesses. ... 41
- Spiritually eliminate all demonic presences and or negative spirits and or vampires and or entities that attempt to negatively affect the system. ... 41
- If a target is able to affect the system in a negative way then the witness is eliminated. ... 42
- Saint Benedict's Sigil ... 43
- Shungite ... 44

Chapter 7 - Contact the Author ... 45

Chapter 8 – Other Resources ... 46

- Kelly Research Technologies ... 46
- All Saints Church Ministry. ... 47
- Twisted Sage – (www.twistedsage.com) Source of Tensor Rings ... 47
- Amazon.com UXCEL 6.7" X 3.1" Blue Metal Enclosure Project Case DIY Junction Box $21.29 ... 48
- Amazon.com Amazon Basics USB 3.0 Extension Cable – A-Male to A-Female 9.8 Feet $6.49 ... 48
- Amazon.com 10 Pack CESS Terminal Binding Post Power Audio Amp Plug Banana Jack $6.79 ... 49
- Amazon.com United Scientific WBP024-PK/6 Banana Plug Cord with Two-Way Stackable $14.53 ... 49
- Conshohocken Radionics. ... 50
- Dan Tuck's Manufacturer of Parcel Designed Thea Lamp and other useful devices. http://www.dtlightworks.com ... 50

Chapter 9 - Bonus Material ... 51

Radionics Reference Books ... 52

Other Books by Peter V. Radatti ... 54

Chapter 1 -
Preface and Dedication

Preface

Radionics is fun. There is always some new problem to investigate and some new radionics program or device to invent or discover! This small booklet is intended to teach how to build an electronic witness well for use with KRT and other radionics machines. While I have not tested it yet, I do believe that the flat plate converter discussed in my book Level-2 Radionics will allow the E-Well to work with the Spooky2 Rife machine's Remove broadcast adaptor.

There are some interesting things you can do with a well of this type, the most interesting are radionics programs that can be transmitted to a target 24-hours/day. Consider programs that provide spiritual protection, spiritual repair, blessings, and enhanced luck. Consider a bubble of protection that reforms instantly upon breaking. Think about blessings such as Kiss of God (35.5-21.4) or the Ho'Oponopono Prayer (51.75-97 & 14-12.25 & 82.75-39) being received 24-hours per day! What would be the value of constant spiritual strengthening such as Soul Integration Repair or Spiritual Vampire Repellent? Basically, anything that cannot be over balanced can be considered for broadcast.

An E-Well cannot be used for everything, in fact there is a lot you cannot do with it, and it is not a way to shotgun a problem but it is a subtle method of great potential which adds a new tool to our already vast tool box of Radionics.

This book assumes that you already understand radionics and have, at a minimal, read the book, "A Fun Course in Beginning Radionics Third Edition: Miracles in the palms of your hands" by the same author. That book is available on www.amazon.com. Search for the author's name of Radatti to locate easily.

This book is not intended as a substitute for the medical advice of physicians. The reader should regularly consult a physician in matters relating to his/her health and, in particular, with respect to any symptoms that may require diagnosis or medical attention. If you think you may be suffering from any medical condition, you should seek immediate medical attention. You should never delay seeking medical advice, disregard medical advice, or discontinue medical treatment because of information in this book.

Peter V. Radatti
April 2017

Preface Update

It took a long time, but something finally got through the protections in the E-Well system. A demon was able to contaminate the system and affect several of the witnesses. They did not infect the witnesses' target but were able to make them miserable and then drain off energy. This update to the book resolves that issue.

Peter V. Radatti
December 2020

Dedication

This book is dedicated to my parents, Marie D. Radatti and Vincent J. Radatti, and to my Aunts and Uncles and friends. These people made me who I am. To the divine spirit who made all possible, including the miracle of life. *Additional Thanks to My Patron Saints:* Saint Jude Thaddeus, Mother Mary, Saint Rita. Finally, this book is dedicated to you my readers. May the knowledge contained herein help you to avoid some of the pain I experienced due to its inaccessibility.

Chapter 2 –
Copyright, ISBN and Legal Notices

Copyright Notice and Editions

Second Edition - Copyright December 2020 © By Peter V. Radatti. All rights reserved.
First Edition - Copyright © By Peter V. Radatti April 2017. All rights reserved.

All rights reserved under United States law and International law, including, but not limited to, the Berne Convention. This work is not in the public domain.

ISBN-13: 978-1545124819

ISBN-10: 1545124817

The first book in this series is:
A Fun Course in Beginning Radionics Third Edition: Miracles in the palms of your hands. ISBN-13: 978-1542419970, ISBN-10: 1542419972

The second book in this series is:
"How to Build an Electronic Witness Well for Radionics". This book

The third book in this series is:
Level-2 Radionics   ISBN: 9798683507800

"Mastering Radionics Series" is a trademark of Peter V. Radatti.

10 9 8 7 6 5 4 3 2

DISCLAIMER

This book is being presented to the reader for informational purposes only. It is meant to assist the general public in learning about the spiritual art known as Radionics. Nothing in this book is intended to serve as legal, medical, scientific, or spiritual advice in *any* matter; it is for educational purposes *only*. Each reader will and must draw their own unique conclusions about the material presented in this book, and if the reader attempts to implement said material, that is entirely their responsibility.

The information provided in this book is designed to provide helpful information on the subjects discussed. It is *not* meant to be used, nor *should* it be used, to diagnose or treat any medical condition; this is the sole purview of your physician. The publisher and author are not responsible for any specific health or allergy needs that may require medical supervision and are not liable for any damages or negative consequences from any treatment, action, application, or preparation to any person reading or following the information in this book. References are provided for informational purposes only and do *not* constitute endorsement of any websites or other sources. Readers should be aware that the websites listed in this book may change.

This book is not intended as a substitute for the medical advice of physicians. The reader should regularly consult a physician in matters relating to his/her health and, in particular, with respect to any symptoms that may require diagnosis or medical attention. If you think you may be suffering from any medical condition, you should seek immediate medical attention. You should never delay seeking medical advice, disregard medical advice, or discontinue medical treatment because of information in this book.

Without prejudice to the generality of the foregoing paragraph, we do not represent, warrant, undertake or guarantee:

that the information in the book is correct, accurate, complete or non-misleading;

that the use of the guidance in the book will lead to any particular outcome or result; or

in particular, that by using the guidance in the book you will have any result.

If a section of this disclaimer is determined by any court or other competent authority to be unlawful and/or unenforceable, the other sections of this disclaimer continue in effect. If any unlawful and/or unenforceable section would be lawful or enforceable if part of it were deleted, that part will be deemed to be deleted, and the rest of the section will continue in effect.

Nothing in this paper should be considered medical advice. For the treatment of any medical condition you must seek the advice of a trained medical doctor.

Chapter 3 –
How to Build an E-Well

The concept of an electronic witness well came from several different people. The first was from an article in the KRT Newsletter written by Ed Kelly. (http://www.kellyresearchtech.com/) This article spoke about different types of witnesses and their effectiveness. Another article was written by me and was on composite witnesses or how to create a witness when you could not get a photo, blood or hair sample. Finally, various radionics operators spoke about how they treat many animals or plants at the same time using a witness of many targets or many witnesses of multiple targets. Many of these discussions were held at the annual All Saints Radionics Masters Conference in Rapid City, SD.

There are many ways of developing an electronic witness well. The simplest electronic witness well is to put witnesses on flash memory such as a thumb-drive and drop the memory in the radionics machine's witness well. Make sure you dowse to ensure the witness is effective. I present a more complex and I believe more powerful E-Well here. This is the unit that I built and am using. Please modify the design to suite your needs.

Why an electronic witness well? Basically, I have several machines, some of which provide balancing 24-hours/day, 7-days/week for one target. This is wasteful so a method where a common radionics program could be sent to thousands of targets at the same time using only one machine would free up resources. This is not unusual. I have seen operators using large witness wells with hundreds of photos as the target.

One method that I used and still use to broadcast without using an expensive radionics machine is an inexpensive primitive radionics machine called a Radionics Power Pod (RPP). While primitive, they work. There are no dials, so an RPP can only be used with preprogrammed crystals. To build your own RPP place a dual spin coil such as the Kelly Betar antenna in a tensor ring. You can buy tensor rings from both of these companies: http://twistedsage.com/ and http://www.dtlightworks.com/. The RPP works but is not as powerful as an actual powered and operating radionics machine.

Building an E-Well is simple and incorporates an RPP as part of the design. The parts list, in no order, is:

1. Steel cabinet or box
2. High quality USB thumb-drive (AKA: Jump Drive, Flash Drive. Plastic, not metal.)

How to Build an Electronic Witness Well for Radionics

3. 20 AWG copper magnet wire. Magnet wire is just copper wire that is coated in thin lacquer instead of plastic installation. This wire is what is used to create the electromagnet in transformers and other devices.
4. Kelly Dual Spin Betar Coil
5. Tensor ring
6. Banana plug jacks
7. A small piece of wood or plastic that fits on the floor of the cabinet
8. A USB extension cable
9. Hot Glue
10. Crazy Glue
11. Sand or crushed gemstones for programming
12. Container for the sand.
13. Banana plug cables to connect the E-Well to a radionics machine.

Using hot glue attach the Radionics Power Pod (Betar coil and Tensor ring) to the piece of wood. See picture below. I purchased a piece of scrap ¼-inch plywood at the hardware store for $0.75. Underlayment (a type of very thin plywood) or a piece of plastic will work well. At the worse, cut the plastic lid from a coffee can to fit the bottom of the cabinet. Leave the KRT Betar coil in the protective plastic box it comes in. It will be sealed by the hot glue.

Open the steel cabinet and glue the wood base with the power pod to the bottom of the cabinet. It is important that you use a steel cabinet. Alternating layers of iron and carbon make an orgone accumulator. Steel is iron and wood or plastic is carbon. A single layer of iron and carbon is a weak but generating orgone accumulator. Never use aluminum. Aluminum and carbon create a negative orgone accumulator also known as a DOR (Dead Orgone) accumulator. In addition to being an orgone accumulator I want to insulate the Radionics Power Pod from conductivity with the steel base. The wood/plastic block does this well.

How to Build an Electronic Witness Well for Radionics

Purchase a very high-quality USB thumb-drive (AKA Jump Drive, Flash Drive). This is of critical importance. Inexpensive or novelty thumb-drives have a high rate of bit-rot. This means that the witnesses will degrade over time. I have personal experience with bit-rot, and it is aggravating. At this time USB 3.0 capable drives are normally of high quality since the higher speed requires that better quality components be used. Fast USB ports are called USB 3.1 (Gen 2). (There are even faster versions, but they require newer computers.) If you can find one of these it will use the high-quality memory. Notice in the photo below it specifies USB 3.0. This is not a 3.1 device but is still high quality.

Basically, purchase a name brand, buy the highest speed that will work with your computer and do not buy cheap. You will notice in the photo below that I paid $10.99 for the Toshiba drive. At the same store, a low-quality USB 2.0 drive of the same size sold for $7.99 and a low quality USB 3.0 drive of the same size sold for $9.99. I paid only $1 more but got high quality. <u>Purchase only plastic drives. Do not purchase a metal drive.</u> At the time I purchased my drive, Toshiba and Samsung made good drives. If you are unsure consult an expert.

How to Build an Electronic Witness Well for Radionics

How many radionics operators does it take to change a light bulb? Answer, none. They just balance the bulb until it works again. - Pete Radatti

Radionics: The art of smile and dial. - Unknown

Did you hear about the radionics razor blade? The company went out of business, they were only able to sell one to a customer. - Pete Radatti

Using the copper magnet wire, carefully wind it around the working part of the thumb-drive. Do not cover any of the USB plug. Make sure it is as tight to the drive as possible. The wire should also be as close to each coil as possible but small mistakes are fine. See the photo below. No specific number of turns are required if the drive body is covered. Leave long tails on the wire and using sandpaper or a knife remove the lacquer from the ends of the tails.

Drill two holes in the front plate of the cabinet large enough to fit the banana plug jacks. Mount the jacks into the holes and tighten the locking nuts in place. Attach the tails of the coil that you sanded from the thumb-drive to the wire lock downs on the inside of the banana plug jacks.

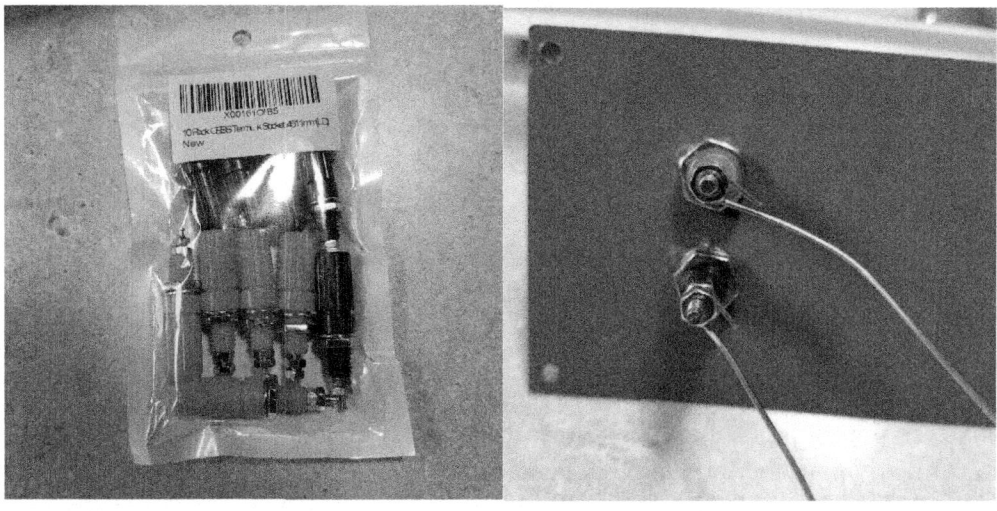

How to Build an Electronic Witness Well for Radionics

This is what the assembly looks like once you are done:

Reattach the front of the cabinet to the cabinet and bend the wire tails so the thumb-drive is centered over the Betar Coil. Here is a picture of the assembly before the tails are bent into place. You can also wait for this step until after you are done gluing inside of the cabinet. It is all a matter of how comfortable you are with tools.

Next fill a container with sand or crushed semi-precious gemstones. I prefer quartz crystal sand however crushed gemstones are the gold standard that have been proven by the test of time. Gemstones never lose their programming. Notice that the box is mostly filled and that all the bottom is covered. It is not necessary or easy to completely fill the box. If the bottom of the box is always covered, you have enough sand. I used one of the boxes a KRT Betar Coil came in. Since sand is so small and fluid, I seal the box using crazy glue. That is not as simple as it sounds. Measure out the sand in the box then pour it into a cup. Wash the plastic box out and thoroughly dry. This will remove static buildup. Quickly pour the sand into the center of the box and close the lid. It should close easily. Once closed hold it sideways and check there is enough sand. Then using a tube of crazy glue seal the place where the lid and the bottom of the box meets. This will keep the sand from coming out. You can also use hot glue but that tends to be messy.

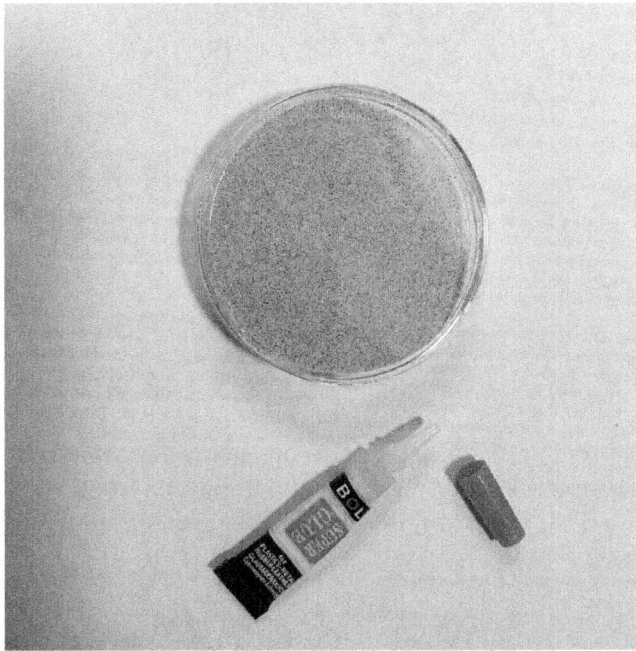

Once the box is sealed program it in your Radionics machine. Use the potentizer well. Use the supplied programs in the back of this book. Unlock the sand. Since it has never been locked this clear it. Program in the ROSP Version 1 program followed by the Hell Burner Version 1 program. Once done, lock the sand using the supplied lock program. These rates will protect the entire system including the E-Well and the radionics system. At the same time these rates will be broadcast to the witnesses 24-hours/day 7-days/week even when turned off.

Do not worry about making changes in the future. You can unlock and change the programs in the sand/gems without removal from the E-Well.

Using a hot glue gun attach the box with the sand/gems to the top of the Radionics Power Pod. Only glue it in three spots but use a large amount. This is so if you ever want to change the program medium you can use a knife to cut the glue and remove the box.

How to Build an Electronic Witness Well for Radionics

You can also program the sand/gems after the system has been assembled. If you ever want to change the programs in the sand, take the lid off of the cabinet and put the entire E-Well inside of a large potentizer well. You can now unlock and add programs or clear the sand and reprogram. Do not forget to lock again when done. (Make a backup copy of the thumb-drive before you do this.)

Position the thumb-drive with cable on the top and center of the sand box. Glue the thumb-drive and coil to the top of the sand box. Only glue it on the sides so you can use a knife to cut the drive away if you ever decide to upgrade the drive. Make sure the cable is attached to the thumb-drive before gluing or you may have a problem attaching it after the glue hardens. Buy a few small tie-wraps. In the photo below (left) the tie-wrap is orange in color. Also buy a few tie-wrap tie-downs. In the picture below it is the white plastic square with the perforated disk on top. The tie-wrap goes though the tie-wrap tie-down. The tie-down has double sided tape on the back. Attach it someplace logical in the box and tie the USB cable down to it using the tie-wrap. (Photo right) This provides strain relief to the thumb-drive. (The strain relief may not be needed depending upon the cabinet strain relief device.)

How to Build an Electronic Witness Well for Radionics

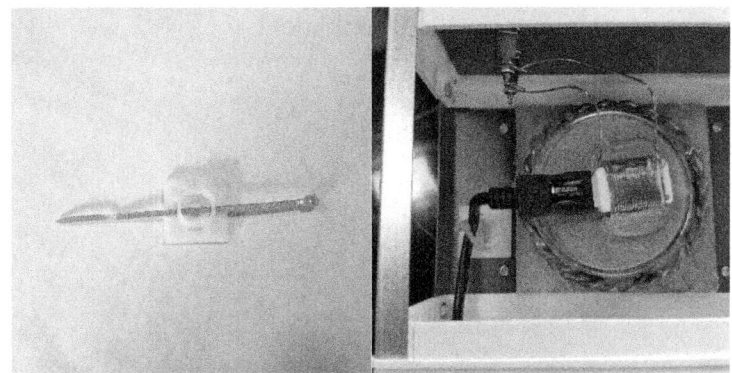

Drill a hole in the back of the cabinet large enough to fit the USB extension cable though. Connect the cable to the thumb-drive. Attach a strain relief to the cable so it does not move the drive when the cable is used. There are many different types of strain relief, choose one that will work for you.

Close the cabinet and attach the banana plug cables. Photo left is a package of banana cables. Photo right is the E-Well with the cables attached to the front and to the INPUT jacks of a KRT Ag Workstation.

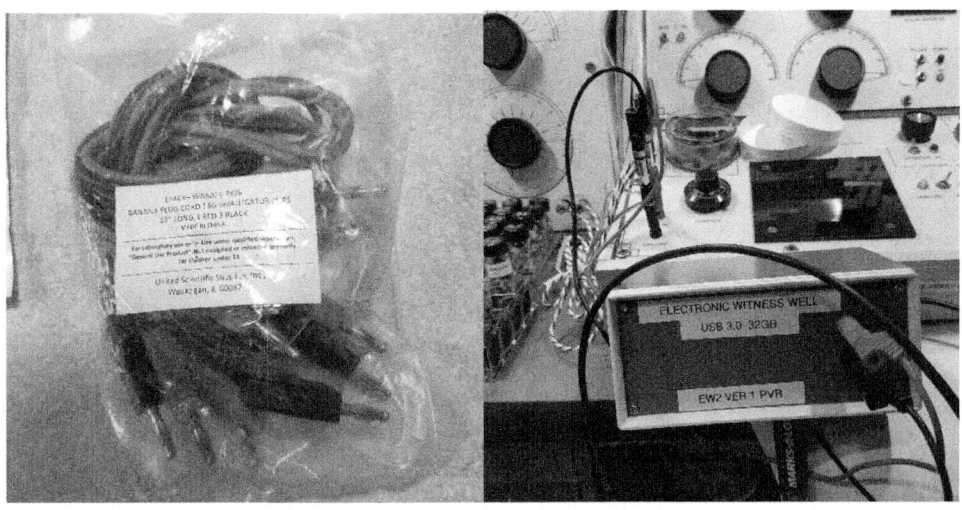

How to Build an Electronic Witness Well for Radionics

Attach a label to the front of the cabinet to make it look nice!

You are now ready to program the witness well with digital witnesses. Any photograph of a target that is at least 5 megapixels or higher will work. You may also want to enter a document with the photograph that further enhances the witness. (Composite witness) Basically any file format will work if you dowse for effectiveness first. Put the file sample on a thumb-drive and enter it in the witness well. Then dowse for a yes/no answer to the question, "Will this witness be effective enough to work for my intended purposes both now and in the future?". If you get a Yes, then proceed. If you get a NO, then you need to add information until you get to a YES. Examples of information is name, address, etc. Anything that clearly identifies the target and only that target.

A 5-megapixel photo is 2580 X 2048 pixels. This is 5.28 Megapixels. Picture file formats at this size will take up the following size in storage:

UNCOMPRESSED FORMATS

TIFF Monochrome 8bit/pixel	5.28 MB
RAW/DNG 10 bits/pixel	6.60 MB
RAW/DNG 12 bits/pixel	7.93 MB
RAW/DNG 14 bits/pixel	9.25 MB
RAW/DNG 16 bits/pixel	10.6 MB
BMP RGB 3x8 bit/pixel	15.9 MB
TIFF CMYK 4x8 bit/pixel	21.1 MB

How to Build an Electronic Witness Well for Radionics

COMPRESSED FORMATS

JPG 100% 24 bit/pixel	1.08 MB
JPG 90% 24 bit/pixel	539 KB
GIF 8 bit/pixel, 255 colors	1.60 MB
PNG lossless 24 bit/pixel	3.07 MB
Lossless JPEG	7.93 MB

If we assume the TIFF format at 21.1 MB and a 32GB thumb-drive which is 32,000 MB, then 32,000 divided by 21.1 MB/photo is a bit over 1,516 photos per drive. If we add a composite witness and assume a small text file with every photo you should easily fit over 1,250 witnesses in the well. That means you can balance 1,250 targets at the same time using a single high-quality radionics machine like a KRT personal workstation. If we assume the more common 24bit JPG format at 1.08MB each we can fit 29629 photos. Leaving lots of space for a composite witness you could store more than double the number of witnesses or about 2,500.

Since the number of witnesses that can be stored in the E-Well is very high there are precautions that you should take to protect your targets. One is to separate each target in the well. Use a separate directory for each witness. For example, lets says I want to put all my pets into the well. I have Bebe the goat, Josie the pussycat[1], Howard the dog and Bubbles the goldfish. I would create a directory of each of their names and put the witness or composite witness into the appropriate directory. While the witnesses are only separated by directory names this separation is effective. There is no cross talk between witnesses. You may want to further organize these directories for ease of management. For example, I have each of these directories in my family directory. It makes it easy and fast for me to find things by organizing data in this way.

In general if you want to delete a witness from the E-Well you can overwrite it with a file of equal or larger size then delete it or you can use one of the super-delete programs available for purchase. This may or may not be important but always better to be safe than sorry. Generally, when you delete a file from a computer it is not actually removed but just marked as deleted and the space made available for reuse. The data could last for a long time before being reused.

---

1 Insider joke for those that grew up watching the cartoon "Josie and the Pussycats".
   https://en.wikipedia.org/wiki/Josie_and_the_Pussycats_(TV_series)

How to Build an Electronic Witness Well for Radionics

Here is a sample form that you can use to create a composite witness:

Name _____ Date _____

Street Address _____

City _____ State _____ Zip Code _____

Phone # (if appropriate) _____

Date of Birth _____

Anything else that can help focus the target. Example, birthmarks, eye color, hair color, etc….

_____   _____

_____   _____

Connect the E-Well to the witness well input jacks on your system and you are ready to go.

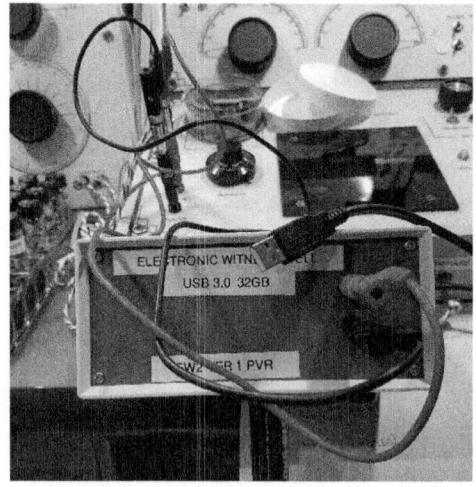

Chapter 4 -
How to use and suggested usage

1. Put all the witnesses you want on the device. Follow directions for separation of witnesses.

2. Connect the output banana plugs from the E-Well to the Input (Witness) jacks on your machine.

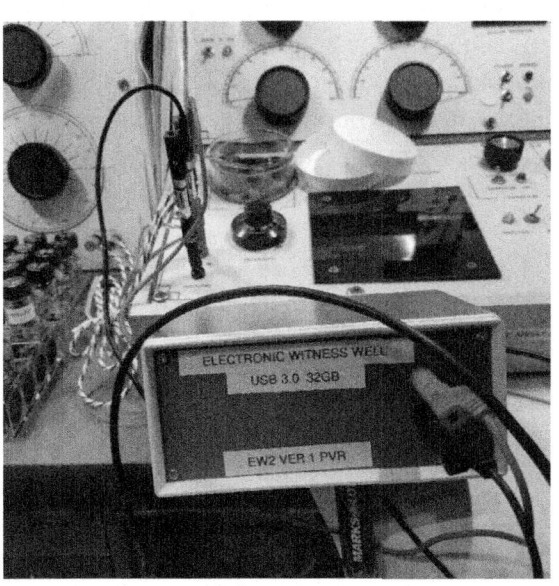

3. Determine what programs you want to broadcast and determine how long you want to broadcast. I strongly suggest you pick programs that can be broadcast 24-hours per day, 7-days per week. Things that cannot be over broadcast are generally blessings and protections. Not all forms of protection are appropriate. Use stick and dowse for what can and cannot be sent. Several of the programs that I developed can be sent in this way. An example is the Soul Integration Repair (SIR). It will have no effect if over broadcast but will repair any deviation as soon as it happens. The same can be said with bubbles of protection, they are safe. If a bubble is destroyed it is reformed. Blessings such as "Kiss of God" 35.5-21.4 cannot be over broadcast. Many but not all, of the rates in VAMPIRE REPELLENT are good for this purpose. Be careful, keep your programs separated into tubes of sand for easy removal and check on everything often.

4. Put the programs you want to broadcast in the witness well. (tubes of sand/gems/crystals) If your witness well is not big enough, I suggest the Large Witness Well sold by KRT. You can also combine programs by potentizing them one at a time into a new tube.

5. Potentizer OFF, Broadcast ON.

That is all there is to it. There is a slight difference between the rates sent by the Radionics Power Pod within the E-Well and what you broadcast via the radionics machine. If you want, and appropriate, you may rebroadcast these.

What results can you expect?

The simple answer is that I have no idea. Everyone reacts differently to balancing. In some cases, people can feel the balancing as warmth or tingling. Most people cannot.

The effect of 24 hour per day balancing is different than a single balancing and you will need to understand this difference and make allowances for it. In many ways, this is an advanced skill. Remember that some people have herxheimer reactions to balancing. A herxheimer reaction is a short term (days to weeks) detoxification reaction. Some of the following symptoms are common: flu-like symptoms, headache, join and muscle pain, body aches, sore throat, general malaise, sweating, chills, nausea or other symptoms.[2] Remember that what we are doing is spiritual and not medical in nature. Things happen based upon a spiritual basis, not a physical basis and are therefore hard to predict.

When the Conshohocken Radionics discussion club tested the E-Well for the first time the following results were noted: (Programs used are unpublished.)

Subject A: Burning stomach, constipation and excessive energy. Difficulty sleeping but no tiredness next day. Coffee consumption reduced from 3 cups to 1 cup. Burning faded in 2 days. General feeling of wellbeing. Fading of some long-term issues.

Subject B: Flu-like symptoms for 2 days. Felt more energetic.

Subject C: Did not notice anything.

Subject D: Excessive energy and difficulty sleeping but no tiredness. Pleased with newfound energy.

Positive symptoms reported including more energy and happiness. Additional test subjects could not be contacted at time of publication. The longer the program runs the more positive symptoms are expected but again, only God knows.

Results will vary according to program used.

---

[2] http://www.silver-colloids.com/Pubs/herxheimer.html

How to Build an Electronic Witness Well for Radionics

When selecting radionics programs to use, be careful in your selection. Use dowsing (stick) to determine if what you want to use is appropriate both now and during the life of the project. Use dowsing to determine if you should add someone to the well or if you need to do manual balancing prior to E-Well balancing. Follow all the rules that you would use if you were to balance a single witness in a machine for 24 hours per day.

Of course, you do not have to use the E-Well 24 hours per day but that is its most powerful use.

Chapter 5 -
Rates used for the E-Well program

I refer to "programs" of stored rates here. They are from my library of public domain radionics "programs/reagents". See Chapter 10 for details. In fact, the entire program you will create from the rates presented is in the library. Details in the chapter.

Unlock-1 (Erase) – Gem Stones / Sand / Solids (no password)

Run Unlock on gems or sand that is not locked and it clears them. Run Unlock once on gems or sand that IS LOCKED and it unlocks them without erasing. Of course, run it twice and you unlock and clear/erase everything.

Unlock potentized Prayer Stones (gems) without changing the primary rates.	68.5-22.6 & 28.75-20.6 & 66.9-34 & 33.5-38.4
	& 57-33.5 & 32-34.5

Lock-1 Gem Stones / Sand / Solids (no password)

This lock allows the frequencies to be copied but not modified, unless they are unlocked. No password is needed. The lock is not copied. Items locked in this way can be run through an airport x-ray machine without damage.

Maximize the potency of all frequencies. (Notes: Scan for appropriateness prior to use.) (All 6 banks are one frequency.)	28.25-31.75 &14-72.25 & 8.5-27.75 &12.5-50.25 & 49.25-42 &43.6-16.6
Lock and protect stones without password	&37.25-11.5

How to Build an Electronic Witness Well for Radionics

Hell Burner 1.0 (from Pete's library)

Potentize gemstones or quartz sand with the ROSP program, Vampire Repellent, Psychic Attack and Sacred Geometry then lock it using Lock-1 Gem.

ROSP Version 1.0

25-27.5	Prepare operator for maximum effectiveness in operating unit and results of operating unit with harm to no one.
27.75-38.75	Prepare unit for proper operation and maximum effectiveness of results with harm to no one.
38.5-58	Clear area of all bad and protect area during operation with harm to no one.
16.1-35 & 3.9-6.9	Install protective bubble of energy around system and operator that allows good energy to flow in and bad energy to flow out but does not allow bad energy in, with harm to no one.
12.00-22.00	White Light
35.5-21.4	Kiss of God.
29.75-6.1 & 2.9-2.5	Clear Witness Well of any impurities
23.9-24.75 & 31.9-11.9 & 9-0	Clear Potentizing Well of any impurities
32.6-33.6 & 16.5-12.9 & 20.25-21.5	Clear Stick Pad of any impurities
22.1-13.9 & 32-17 & 11.5-9.75	Ignore any impurities in Witness that may cause false values.
23.6-8.25 & 8.9-12.5	Enhance Stick for maximum effectiveness and correct answers
52.5-18.2 & 15-16 & 9-15 & 26.9-51.5	All rates entered on this system are modified to be "With Harm To No One".

How to Build an Electronic Witness Well for Radionics

19.75-11.5 & 37.4-17.5 & 17.75-23 & 31.1-21.25	Radionically Diagnose and Repair anything wrong with this unit.
67-27.5 & 31-35.9 & 14.2-27.7	Connect Radionics equipment to God.
59.9-65.5 & 63-50.75 & 89.9-72.5 & 32.9-45	Connect Radionics Operator to God.
60.5-59.5 & 34-49 & 49-24.1 & 42.5-40.6 & 40.5-33.5 & 43.2-54.5	Draw energy from God to power Radionics Operator.
64.5-49 & 33.9-57 & 33-65.4 & 48.5-73 & 37.8-41	Draw energy from God to power Radionics Device.
62-65.5 & 59.5-49.2 & 49-35.25 & 72.5-59.75 &45-50 & 55.4-45.2	Seek divine protection from God during operation of Radionics device.
87.5-58.25 & 70.9-66 & 33.6-46.5 & 66.9-76	Do not allow Radionics Operator's personal life-force to be used in operation.
73-47.2 & 55.5-37 & 53.75-57.7 & 37.5-61.5	Do not allow false readings from minerals
86.5-29.75 & 26.1-38 & 20-56.2 & 52-66.75 & 60.4-52 & 69.9-71 & 75-79.75	Do not allow false readings from environmental issues.
44.9-17 & 11-15.5 & 17-15 & 22.9-18.6 & 12.75-15 & 24-27.5	Do not allow false readings from energetic issues.

VAMPIRE REPELLENT

Start with spiritual first aid:
1. KRT   Cords, Release All   39.5-25.5
       Needed cords reestablish themselves, so this is house cleaning.

How to Build an Electronic Witness Well for Radionics

2. KRT Affirmation, I am surrounded by a strong, white light, 18.5-38.25
I am protected from harm. You will need this, but it is not
complete protection from a vampire.

3. KRT Divine Protection 48-58

4. KRT Gem Obsidian, Deflect Negativity, protection, healing 77.5-71.75

5. KRT Italian Alder, protected peace 70-62

Start the process of spiritual healing:

6. PVR Kiss of God 35.5-21.4

7. PVR To stir the chi in the body. Vampire attacks can cause blocks. 23-23.6

8. PVR Install protective bubble of energy around witness that 16.1-35,3.9-6.9
allows good energy to flow in and bad energy to flow *out*
but does not allow bad energy *in*, with harm to no one.
This is not a total answer because the vampire is taking your
good energy out.

Prevent it from happening again:

9. PVR Install a very sharp, spinning, outer bubble of protection around 77.5-66.6
other bubbles of protection that can cut any unwanted cords or & 10-13.25
attachment that are drawing energy from witness. Notice: This & 21.5-26.25
only eliminates unwanted cords, so if you are in love with the & 36.5-20.6
vampire (common), you will need to decide what you are going & 20.5-45.8
to do. There are healthy cords that exchange energy, so you want
those to reestablish themselves. This bubble is not 100% protection
by itself.

10. PVR Forcefully and continuously break any cords that draw unhealthy 12.5-47
amounts of life-force energy. Notice: This is different from #9 in that &17.5-
34.75it acts as a circuit breaker. There are times you may want to give energy
&69.25-50.4
but not at the cost of your spiritual health. & 31.75-35

How to Build an Electronic Witness Well for Radionics

			& 39.5-63 & 64.5-82.6 & 38.5-59.4
11.	EAA	Ho'Oponopono Prayer	51.75-97 & 14-12.25 & 82.75-39
12.	PVR	Become repugnant to vampires This is a difficult one to implement, therefore the large number of rates. In addition, this is not proof by itself. It will make the target repugnant in the same way that cooked liver and spinach are repugnant to some small children. Be 91.2 when setting the rates. You may break up the rates into batches, but they are all one rate. If you break them up, rescan time for each batch.	50-23.9 & 23-33 68.9-58.1 & 27.26-5.25 27.8-73.4 & 23.8-12 36.5-38.4 & 15.6-16.5 57.1-44.75 & 14.5- 45.2-27.2 & 48.75-22.9

Reestablish proper and healthy connection to life-force:

13.	KRT	Angelic Support, Connect with divine guidance	36.5-35.5
14.	KRT	Attunement with God	21-37
15.	KRT	Affirmation, Worthy of and joyously receive and use continuously an abundance of God's loving	26-28.5 & 25.5-10.5
16.	PVR	Reattach to Universal Life-force / God. This rate is very useful for everything, not just Vampires. Everything in existence needs a connection to God. Ensure that the connection always exists. You can balance this rate.	98-71 & 35.5-22 20-5 & 3.25-22.5 50.8-98.25 & 65-54.4

Soul Integration Repair Protocol

(SIR)

THIS IS IMPORTANT! The Spirit creates the Astral Body. The Astral Body creates the Physical Body. There are a lot of steps involved, but we know that Information Transfer is a critical part of that process. To a certain extent, you can consider that the transfer method for information is a type of circuit. While not the entire process, this attempts to correct any damage to the transfer and control circuits of the Soul that build the Astral and Physical bodies. The Soul projects the Physical body; it does not occupy it. Explanation: Many people think that the physical body is like a jar, and it contains the soul. That is incorrect. The soul projects the physical body in much the same way that a movie projector projects an image. The physical body is just an extension of the soul, and a weak one at that. If you are attempting to balance these, you want as high an Intensity as possible, always much higher than GV. It is appropriate to put these rates in jewelry. In addition, check White Light and balance, if necessary, with Psychic Attack.

This is also one of the ways that demons and negative entities gain entrance to the Astral Body and the Physical Body. Repair of the damage at the entry points makes it very difficult for these entities to attack.

IMPORTANT NOTE: Any rate marked with an asterisk is an entry point for demons and negative entities. You must check, then triple check your settings. The rate needs to be checked often if psychic attack is suspected. The critical value of the RHD rate will be specified in each case. This rate must be exact. Since it is a critical rate, you should always check for appropriateness and harm to no one. Better safe than sorry. All potentization times will vary.

Soul-to-Astral

Soul-to-Astral Primary Information Circuit

This is 1 rate on 3 banks.
Potentize into gems for 6 minutes.

61.4-21.5 &
22.5-25.6 &
7.5-62.25

Soul-to-Astral Secondary Information Circuit

This is 1 rate on 4 banks.
Potentize into gems for 11 minutes.

38.9-9 &
58.75-78 &
66.75-17 &
17.5-28.4

How to Build an Electronic Witness Well for Radionics

Soul-to-Astral Third Information Circuit

This is 1 rate on 3 banks.
Potentize into gems for 37 minutes.

    33.9-87.6 &
    52-70.4 &
    22-60.5

Soul-to-Astral Fourth Information Circuit

This is 2 rates on 5 banks. The first rate takes 2 banks. The second rate takes 3 banks.
Potentize the first rate into gems for 14 minutes.

    100-49.5 &
    16-17.6

Potentize the second rate into gems for 21 minutes.

    34.5-14.9 &
    71.4-37.75 &
    57.75-35.75

Soul-to-Astral Fifth Information Circuit

This is 3 rates on 11 banks.
Potentize the first rate into gems for 32 minutes.

    30.5-88 &
    97-90 &
    16.5-15.5

Potentize the second rate into gems for 42 minutes.

    90.25-62.7 &
    56-59.25 &
    97.75-76 &
    16.5-23.9 &
    28.75-98.9

Potentize the third rate into gems for 13 minutes.

    28.75-99 &
    14.5-18.75 &
    15.1-17.5 &
    13.25-17.25

Soul-to-Astral Sixth Information Circuit

This is 1 rate on 3 banks.
Potentize this rate into gems for 16 minutes.

    39.5-33 &
    11-13 &
    37.75-39

How to Build an Electronic Witness Well for Radionics

Soul-to-Astral Seventh Information Circuit

This is 1 rate on 5 banks.
Potentize this rate into gems for 25 minutes.

    82.4-30.75 &
    13-52.25 &
    12.5-38 &
    20.25-12.75 &
    27.8-12.4

Soul-to-Astral Eighth Information Circuit (CRITICAL RATE)

This is 2 rates on 6 banks. (CRITICAL RATE)
Potentize the first rate into gems for 9 minutes.

    24-28.75 &
    13.75-45.75 &
    27.75-29 &
    9-25

Potentize the second rate into gems for 5 minutes. IMPORTANT NOTE: This rate is one of the entry points for demons and negative entities. This rate needs to be checked often if psychic attack is suspect. The critical value is the RHD rate of 14.5.   14.9-14.5 &

    15.75-6.6

Soul-to-Astral Ninth Information Circuit

This is 3 rates on 4 banks. (CRITICAL RATE)
Potentize the first rate into gems for 13 minutes.

    44-56.1 &
    28.5-28

Potentize the second rate into gems for 10 minutes.   43.25-39.9

Potentize the third rate into gems for 7 minutes. IMPORTANT NOTE: This rate is also an entry point for demons and negative entities. This rate needs to be checked often if psychic attack is suspect. The critical value is the RHD rate of 12.5   38.4-12.5

Soul-to-Astral Tenth Information Circuit

This is 4 rates on 4 banks. (CRITICAL RATE)
Potentize the first rate into gems for 14 minutes.   78.1-30.25

Potentize the second rate into gems for 16 minutes.   74.25-39.9

Potentize the third rate into gems for 13 minutes.   24.25-26

Potentize the fourth rate into gems for 18 minutes. IMPORTANT NOTE: This rate is also an entry point for demons and negative entities. This rate needs to be checked often if psychic attack is suspect. The critical value is the RHD rate of 15.2.   37.5-15.2

How to Build an Electronic Witness Well for Radionics

Astral to Physical

Astral To Physical Primary Information Circuit

This is 3 rates on 7 banks. (CRITICAL RATE)
Potentize the first rate into gems for 19 minutes.   53-38 &
19.5-13.4

Potentize the second rate into gems for 15 minutes.   88-44.75 &
25-68.25

Potentize the third rate into gems for 6 minutes. IMPORTANT NOTE: This rate is also an entry point for demons and negative entities. This rate needs to be checked often if psychic attack is suspect. The critical value is the RHD rate of 14.6   34-14.6 &
34-18.25 &
19.5-35.25

Astral To Physical Secondary Information Circuit

This is 3 rates on 3 banks.
Potentize the first rate into gems for 4 minutes.   15.1-42

Potentize the second rate into gems for 11 minutes.   54.5-10.25

Potentize the third rate into gems for 20 minutes.   42-22.75

Astral To Physical Third Information Circuit

This is 3 rates on 3 banks.
Potentize the first rate into gems for 19 minutes.   49.25-31

Potentize the second rate into gems for 16 minutes.   43.5-35.75

Potentize the third rate into gems for 19 minutes.   22.75-31.5

Astral To Physical Fourth Information Circuit

This is 3 rates on 5 banks.
Potentize the first rate into gems for 17 minutes.   34.25-8.5 &
9.5-94 &
51.25-44.5

Potentize the second rate into gems for 17 minutes   97.5-38.25

Potentize the third rate into gems for 13 minutes.   24.4-38.6

Astral To Physical Fifth Information Circuit

This is 3 rates on 5 banks.

Potentize the first rate into gems for 9 minutes.   58.4-33.6 &
                                                       18-21   &
                                                       15.1-13

Potentize the second rate into gems for 11 minutes. This is an important rate (RHD) but it is unknown why.   41-27.9

Potentize the third rate into gems for 13 minutes. This is an important rate (RHD) but it is unknown why.   26.5-18.7

Astral To Physical Sixth Information Circuit

This is 2 rates on 4 banks.

Potentize the first rate into gems for 16 minutes.   46.75-38.4 &
                                                       35.5-26.75 &
                                                       25-19.75

Potentize the second rate into gems for 19 minutes. Time will vary. This is an important rate, especially the RHD value of 13.25, but it is unknown why.   25.7-13.25

Astral To Physical Seventh Information Circuit

This is 2 rates on 4 banks.

Potentize the first rate into gems for 8 minutes.   26.6-17.5 &
                                                       8.5-14

Potentize the second rate into gems for 11 minutes.   27.1-21.9 &
                                                       13.25-30.25

Astral To Physical Eighth Information Circuit

This is 2 rates on 3 banks.

Potentize the first rate into gems for 15 minutes.   70.4-66 &
                                                       17.5-45.5

Potentize the second rate into gems for 13 minutes.   35-36.75

Astral To Physical Ninth Information Circuit

This is 4 rates on 7 banks.

Potentize the first rate into gems for 20 minutes.   32.5-13.25 & 20-5.25

Potentize the second rate into gems for 22 minutes.   17.4-27.6 19-19.25

Potentize the third rate into gems for 29 minutes. This is an important rate, especially the RHD value of 7.5, but it is unknown why.   27.5-7.5 & 16.5-10.75

Potentize the fourth rate into gems for 11 minutes.   31.25-15

Astral To Physical Tenth Information Circuit

This is 2 rates on 3 banks.

Potentize the first rate into gems for 28 minutes.   34-27.5 & 19-25.75

Potentize the second rate into gems for 23 minutes.   22-23

Soul-to-Astral-to-Physical Basic Structure

There is basic information that defines an Astral and Physical body. Without this basic information, an Astral body would not be an Astral body; it would be something else. If this information becomes damaged, then it must be repaired. These rates are for humans only. The Soul, also known as the Spirit, is. It exists in perpetuity. It cannot be truly damaged, but it *can* collect negative stuff that does not allow it to project properly. Think of this process as burying a light in dirt. It is still bright, but no one can see it under all the dirt. If the dross on your soul is severe enough, then you just would not exist because you could not project the next level toward a physical body. Without a Soul, everything else is moot. The fact that you exist at this physical level is proof that your soul exists. To understand this, I draw upon the parallel Christian concept of original sin or the Buddhist concept of inherited karma. We will attempt to clean the Soul, but very gently. We cannot destroy or modify the Soul, but we do not want to add any dirt, either. The Soul projects the Astral Body. The Astral Body projects the Physical Body. The information flow is bi-directional! Your physical body is much more of a projection than a container.

How to Build an Electronic Witness Well for Radionics

Information that defines the basic structure of an Astral Body

This is 3 rates on 7 banks.
Potentize the first rate into gems for 10 minutes.   9.5-23.9 &
   7-17

Potentize the second rate into gems for 7 minutes.   22.5-10 &
   4.5-9.4

Potentize the third rate into gems for 10 minutes. This is an important rate, especially the RHD values of 18 and 14.4, but it is unknown why.   17.3-18 &
   18.5-14.4 &
   16.5-20.25

Information that defines the basic structure of a Physical Body

This is 1 rate on 5 banks.
Potentize this rate into gems for 29 minutes.   11.5-15.5 &
   12-18.5 &
   12.5-50 &
   16.5-100 &
   25.9-30.25

Removal of Information that Does Not Belong in/on the Soul

This is 1 rate on 4 banks
Potentize this rate into gems for 18 minutes.   37-29.1 &
   16.5-21.9 &
   14.5-37 &
   43-37.5

Removal of Information that damages the transfer of information from the Soul to the Astral Body

This is 1 rate on 7 banks.

Potentize this rate into gems for 11 minutes.   68.4-46 &
   26-24.1 &
   19.5-30.5 &
   20.3-22.25 &
   74.5-34 &
   31.1-25

How to Build an Electronic Witness Well for Radionics

Removal of Information that Does Not Belong in the Astral Body

This is 2 rates on 4 banks.
Potentize the first rate into gems for 14 minutes.   20.75-24.5 &
                                                        28.1-11

Potentize the second rate into gems for 7 minutes.   28.6-30.75 &
                                                        13.5-11

Removal of Information that damages the transfer of information from the Astral to the Physical Body.

This is 5 rates on 7 banks.
Potentize the first rate into gems for 20 minutes.   44.5-12 &
                                                        19-15

Potentize the second rate into gems for 18 minutes.   39.5-16.5 &
                                                        25.9-85.4

Potentize the third rate into gems for 18 minutes. The RHD value of 24.75 and the 18 minutes are critical values, but it is unknown why. Pay close attention to the value while potentizing.
                                                        16.9-24.75

Potentize the fourth rate into gems for 8 minutes. The RHD value of 9.2 is critical but it is unknown why.
                                                        71.9-9.2

Potentize the fifth rate into gems for 18 minutes.   31-77.25

How to Build an Electronic Witness Well for Radionics

Psychic Attack

Psychic Attack

Name:			Sex:			Project Intent:		
Animal Type:			Age:					
Description	Left	Right	Left	Right	Reading	Reading	Reading
Yes/No	100.00-	0.00					
General Vitality	9.00-	49.00					
White Light	12.00-	22.00					

Dark Forces - Associated with directed negative thinking or energy, typically the result of singular emotional bursts rather than a long term attack. These rates usually respond rapidly to balancing, though the stronger the emotional charge, the longer the time to balance. The intensity of White Light should be within 50 of General Vitality. The ratio of White Light to any Dark Forces energy should be 10:1. *Broadcast on rate to reduce any value above 50.*

Description	Left	Right	Left	Right	Reading	Reading	Reading
Dark Force, Negative Thinking, Influences	11.00-	21.00					
Dark Force, Negative Thinking, Influences	11.50-	25.00					
Dark Force, Negative Thinking, Influences	16.00-	1.00					
Dark Force, Negative Thinking, Influences	25.50-	0.50					
Dark Force, Negative Thinking, Emotion, Influences	30.00-	16.00					
Dark Psychic Forces	26.30-	28.50					

Negative Energies - Associated with non-directed negatively charged energies, including vortexes and ley lines generated by the planet. Other forms include old patterns of information bound to a location, as in the case of paranormal activity. *Broadcast on rate to reduce any value above 50.*

Description	Left	Right	Left	Right	Reading	Reading	Reading
Implant Receiving, Psychic Attack Accompanied by Dark Force or Negative Blocking Body	20.00-	37.00					
Interference from Multi-Dimensional, Psychic Attack	57.00-	63.50					
Emotional, Psychic Toxins	10.75-	35.75					
Emotional, Psychic Toxins	16.25-	27.50					
Emotional, Psychic Toxins	17.25-	45.50					
Emotional, Psychic Toxins	25.75-	26.25					
Emotional, Psychic Toxins	26.50-	16.00					
Emotional, Psychic Toxins	36.00-	28.00					
Emotional, Psychic Toxins	38.25-	28.25					
Emotional, Psychic Toxins	42.75-	27.75					
Emotional, Psychic Toxins	26.25-	38.25					
Emotional, Psychic Toxins	46.50-	28.25					
Emotional, Psychic Toxins	55.75-	16.00					
Emotional, Psychic Toxins	56.25-	17.50					
Psychic Numbness	33.50-	32.00					

Killer Psychic Force Rates - These energies are both directed and of a much higher intensity than Dark Forces. They may be the result of extreme emotions, produced by the mentally unstable or the work of structured negativity, including curses, spells or voodoo. These energies may also be introduced by discarnate entities, and this should be taken into account in cases of alcoholism, drug habit (prescribed or recreational), recent emotional stress, and traumatic injury. *Broadcast on rate to reduce any value above 50. Expect longer than average broadcast times.*

Description	Left	Right	Left	Right	Reading	Reading	Reading
Killer Dark Psychic Force	10.25-	34.50					
Killer Dark Psychic Force	11.50-	46.50					
Killer Dark Psychic Force	21.00-	11.00					
Killer Dark Psychic Force	25.00-	21.50					
Killer Dark Psychic Force, Dark Force, Influences	25.50-	scan					
Killer Dark Psychic Force	26.25-	28.50					
Killer Dark Psychic Force, Thinking	39.50-	69.50					
Killer Dark Psychic Force	46.50-	scan					
Killer Dark Psychic Force, Unknown	39.00-	13.00					

This information compiled for *experimental agricultural research only* and is not intended for use with humans. If medical or mental health care is needed, please visit a licensed professional.

Copyright 2012, Kelly Research Technologies, Inc.

How to Build an Electronic Witness Well for Radionics

Psychic Attack

 **Psychic Attack**

Description	Left	Right	Left	Right	Reading	Reading	Reading
Implant Mechanisms - These complex energy patterns are associated with the armoring of the seven major chakra centers, reflecting the relationship between the state of mind and the energetic body of the individual. *Broadcast on rate to reduce for periods ranging from 5 minutes to 4 hours. Monitor closely.*							
1. Negative Entity	36.50-	36.50	21.00-	5.50			
2. Receive Germ broadcast	17.25-	35.25	15.25-	21.25			
3. Reception Control Lines	5.25-	11.25	13.00-	18.00			
4. Adverse Affecting Thought & Emotions	18.25-	36.25	25.25-	28.25			
Also check with scanned locations	34.50-	52.00					
5. Renewing Miasms	20.00-	21.00	35.25-	15.50			
6. May Cause Arthritis	18.25-	23.00	13.25-	27.00			
7. May Cause Cancer	90.25-	90.00	15.50-	28.25			
or	25.00-	58.75	80.50-	48.25			
8. May Induce Aging	0.25-	18.75	31.75-	28.25			
9. May Cause Psychosis	13.00-	23.00	29.00-	33.25			
10. May Cause Insomnia	13.00-	48.00	29.50-	28.50			
11. Affects Assimilation	78.25-	28.00	28.25-	13.00			
12. May Cause Lymph Malfunction	28.25-	73.25	3.00-	95.25			
13. May Cause Physical Malfunction	28.25-	38.25	10.25-	98.25			
or	16.00-	17.75					
14. Siphons White Light	30.25-	18.00	18.25-	98.25			
15. Drains Prana	30.25-	13.25	16.00-	28.25			
16. Splits Auric Levels (important with mind expanding drugs)	28.25-	48.25	58.25-	33.75			
17. May Cause Blood Clots	28.25-	68.25	45.50-	28.25			
or	9.75-	6.25	2.75-	12.25			
18. Malefic Planetary Rays	8.75-	14.25	4.75-	74.00			
19. Interferes with Consciousness	2.25-	21.00	10.75-	63.25			
20. Interferes with the Feeling of Well-Being	11.25-	41.75	60.75-	48.75			
21. Physical Malfunction	26.00-	43.50	72.75-	27.25			
22. Unites Dark Force & Malefic Planetary Rays	38.50-	36.40	32.50-	41.50			
23. Combines Dark Force and Germ Reception	38.75-	32.25	43.50-	27.00			
24. May Damage Eyes	30.75-	34.50	27.00-	32.25			
25. May Cause Colds and flu	41.50-	48.25	39.00-	32.75			
26. May Cause Malignancies	38.50-	48.50	28.00-	16.25			
27. May Cause Malignancies	19.25-	68.00	17.00-	13.25			
28. Dark Forces Implant Receptor	26.00-	63.25	18.25-	47.00			
29. Reduces Susceptibility to Radiation Exposure	58.25-	16.25	22.25-	79.00			
30. May Cause Energy Leakage	28.00-	38.50	17.25-	27.75			
31. May Cause TB	53.50-	57.00	50.50-	38.50			
32. May Cause Implants to Occur	27.75-	12.25	8.75-	52.50			
33. May Cause Greater Susceptibility to Mental Control Mechanisms	72.50-	51.60	49.00-	89.00			

2011-02

This information compiled for *experimental agricultural research only* and is not intended for use with humans. If medical or mental health care is needed, please visit a licensed professional.

Copyright 2012, Kelly Research Technologies, Inc.

Sacred Geometry Shapes and their Rates

Platonic Solids					
Tetrahedron	57.25-27		>800		
Hexahedron	92-99		>800		
Octahedron	55-49.50		>800		
Dodecahedron	20.75-93		>800		
Icosahedron	44.75-79		>800		
Icositetrachoron	93.50-79.25		>800		
Icosahedron-Pentagonal-Dodecahedron	56-60.75	74-87.50	>800		
Phi (Golden Ratio)	88.50-85.25		>800		
Archimedean solids					
Cuboctahedron	34-37.25				
Icosidodecahedron	28.50-95.50				
Rhombicubeoctahedron	95.50-18.25				
Rhombicosidodecahedron	54.50-29.50				
Rhombi truncated Cuboctahedron	6.25-90.25				
Rhombi truncated Icosidodecahedron	52.50-45				
Snub Cube	77.50-83.25				
Snub Dodecahedron	97-50				
Truncated Cube	47.25-63.25				
Truncated Dodecahedron	83-81				
Truncated Icosahedron	13-92				
Truncated Octahedron	54.50-51.50				
Truncated Tetrahedron	70.50-77.25				

Chapter 6 –
New Material for Second Edition

It took a long time, but something finally got through the protections in the E-Well system. A demon was able to contaminate the system and affect several of the witnesses. They did not infect the witnesses' target but were able to make them miserable and then drain off energy.

I was born under the sign of Cancer. If you know what that means, then you know that the demon involved did not escape my fury. At the same time, I was unhappy that the protections failed. I added many new layers of protection and have been running this new version for a long period of time with no problems. As always, the future is unknown so you may need to adjust from time to time.

Isolate all witnesses so that no crosstalk or interaction of any kind is possible.

41.5-41
24.1-23
70-80.9
19-50
11-45.25
26.25-30.75
19.5-66.6
32-27.4
18.5-46.6
76.5-99.75
21-28.4
25-39.9
5.6-24.25

How to Build an Electronic Witness Well for Radionics

Stove pipe all witnesses so that they are delivered to the radionics machine separately without any interaction with other witnesses.

32-31 & 19.75-52.5
71.25-55
20.75-29.5
24.25-28
11-72.5
28.25-51.25
37-93.2
34-27
69.9-93.5
8.5-32.1
67.5-60.1

Spiritually eliminate all demonic presences and or negative spirits and or vampires and or entities that attempt to negatively affect the system.

40-38.4
29-26.5
27-49.25 & 34.25-43
51.75-60.75 & 23.20-56.10
15.5-42.75 & 37-39.1
20.6-81 & 68.7-71
60.20-43.75 & 53.25-33
70-13.1 & 93.5-85.5
14-8.75 & 9.2-21.25
10.75-15 & 26.5-29.5
44.5-37.4 & 47.25-43.25
46.75-48.25 & 66.25-94

How to Build an Electronic Witness Well for Radionics

If a target is able to affect the system in a negative way then the witness is eliminated.

73.25-94 **&** 11.5-3.75
40.5-24.75
35.75-21.5
38.5-29.4
65.1-30.75
60.5-52.25
40.9-20.6
92.5-92.5
14.75-43.50
29.20-46.70
29.75-21.9
30.8-13.25
32.2-43.25
23.6-23.9
32.1-38.25
62-65
71.25-40.75
29-36.5
21.8-32.75
41-24
39.25-27.5
38.75-56.75
28.5-40.5
31.75-39.25
43.5-80.25
76.9-54.75
45.9-27.5
95-61
23.75-55

Saint Benedict's Sigil

Saint Benedict's sigil (reverse side) is used to remove demons and evil spirits. There are several prayers against evil on this sigil in Latin. VRSNSMV means Vade Retro Satana, Nonquam Suade Mihi Vana translated as "Begone Satan, do not suggest to me thy vanities". Followed by SMQLIVB means Sunt Mala Quae Libas, Ipse Venena Bibas translated as "Evil are the things thou proferrest, drink thy own poison".

To understand the remainder of the sigil I recommend the following URL:

https://catholicsaintmedals.com/understanding-the-st-benedict-medal/

Shungite

Shungite is a natural mineral that is mostly carbon. Black or black-grey in color it is prized by spiritual practitioners for its anti-demonic and healing properties. Since the mineral is valuable sellers often attempt to pass off less expensive black rocks as shungite. To test a rock to determine if it is shungite you can test it for conductivity. Shungite is conductive to electricity. If you don't have a meter you can use a battery, flashlight bulb and a jumper wire to test conductivity. If the bulb lights then the mineral is likely shungite.

Chapter 7 - Contact the Author

If you are going to send me spam or hate-mail, please do not. If you are going to explain to me how I am misguided, please do not. If you have questions about what I wrote or have helpful suggestions, feel free to write. If you just want a forum to discuss Radionics, welcome. Telling me to dunk my head in a bucket is not helpful. I tried and did not care for it; the water was too cold.

My email for the purpose of this book is: **peter@tigerteam.com**

If the address gets bombed, I will discontinue it. Then, you might be able to contact me via the

Conshohocken Radionics meetup site: http://www.meetup.com/radionics/

You can also find me on Facebook.

Updates to this and my other books can be found at:

www.radatti.com/books

Click on the book you are interested in and any updates will be available for download.

Thank you for reading my book. I look forward to your questions and comments.

Chapter 8 –
Other Resources

Kelly Research Technologies

There are fantastic training and rate books available free from KRT, who manufactures professional-quality radionics devices. They also sponsor classes. Their website is:

http://www.kellyresearchtech.com

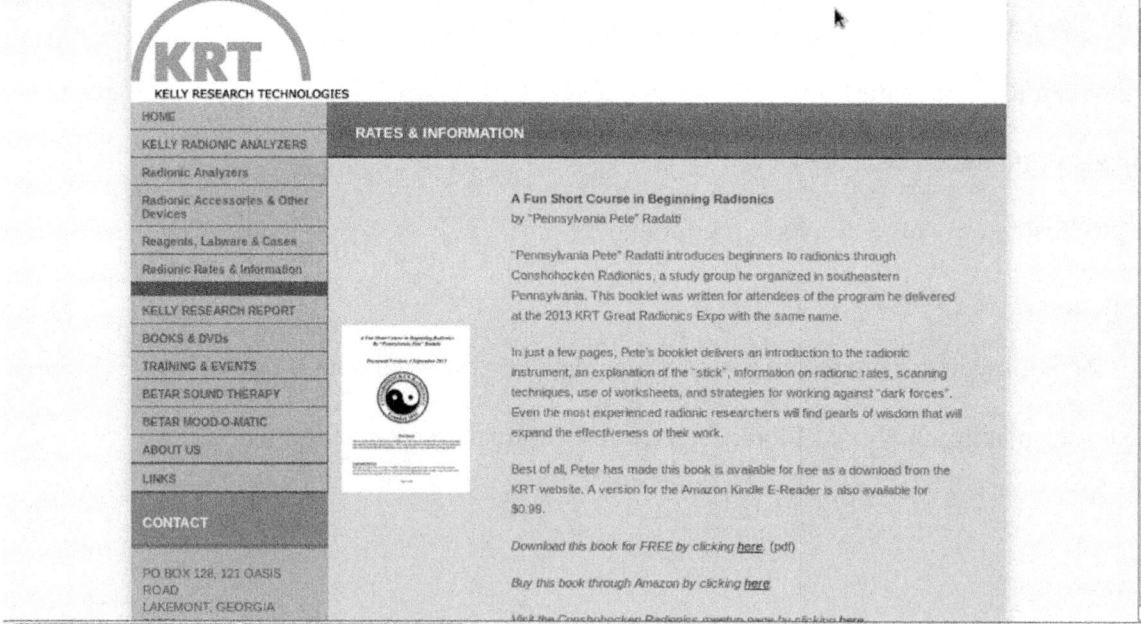

To download Ed Kelly's Radionics books, use the following link:
www.kellyresearchtech.com/download.html

Here are descriptions of the books from KRT's website:

"KRT Radionics Book 2: Applied Radionics

Take control of your energetic destiny with this hands-on manual featuring step-by-step instructions for safe and successful use of all KRT radionic analyzers and potentizers, as well as advanced strategies, techniques, and topics. Much of the information in this book is directly applicable to other two-dial analyzers, including Hieronymus, Rogers, Mattioda, and Lightning devices."

"KRT Radionics Book 3: Radionic Rates - Alpha

This book is the result of more than 35 years of compiling, collecting, and creating radionic rates for two-dial instruments. A reference volume for use in energetic research, this database includes more than 13,800 rates and is sorted alphabetically. Ideal for use with all Kelly instruments, as well as all

Hieronymus, Rogers, Mattioda, Lightning, and SE-5 radionic devices."

All Saints Church Ministry.

Wellness consultations and advanced training in energetics / metaphysics & radionics. For info call 605-787-5620 or email livingwordministry8@yahoo.com

Twisted Sage – (www.twistedsage.com) Source of Tensor Rings

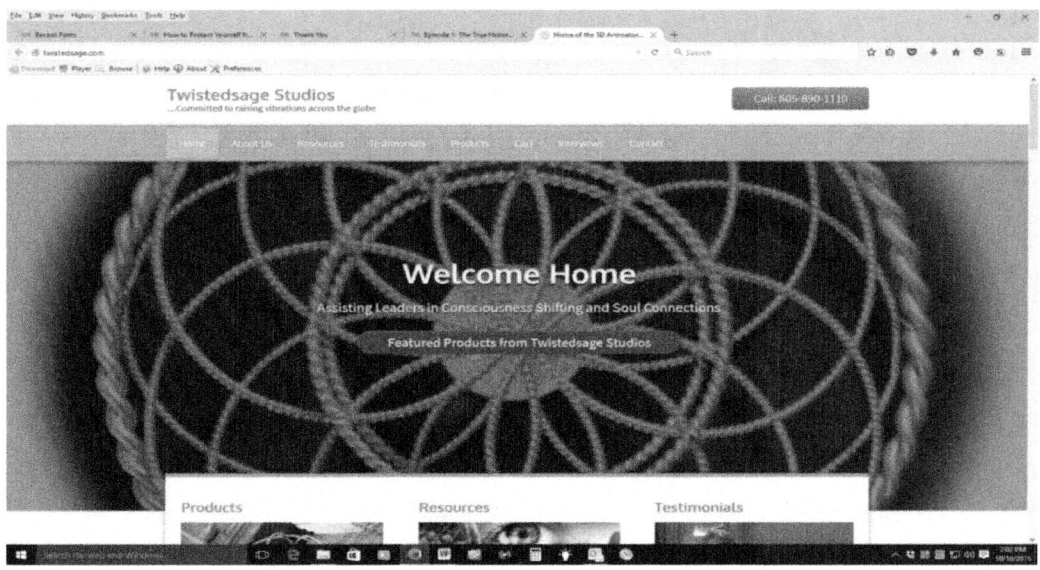

How to Build an Electronic Witness Well for Radionics

Amazon.com UXCEL 6.7" X 3.1" Blue Metal Enclosure Project Case DIY Junction Box $21.29

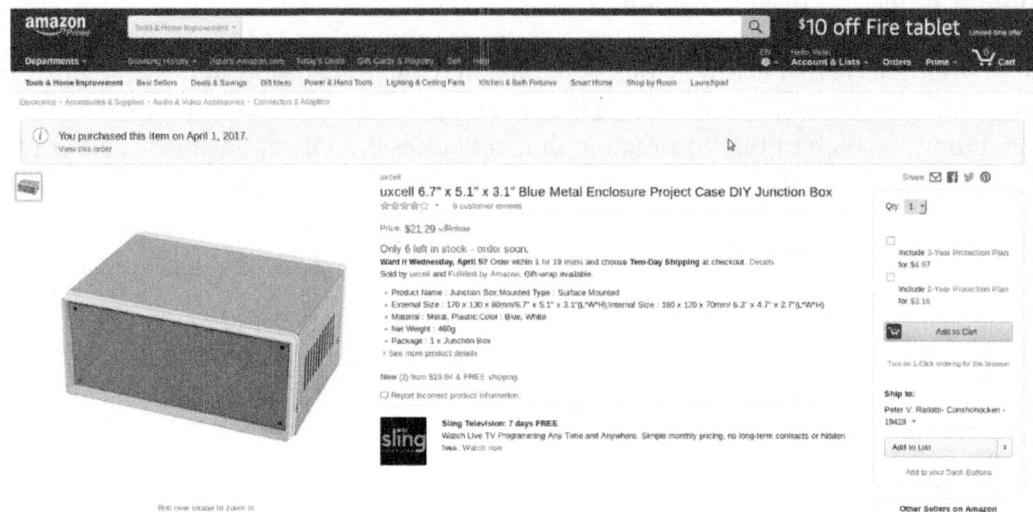

Amazon.com Amazon Basics USB 3.0 Extension Cable – A-Male to A-Female 9.8 Feet $6.49

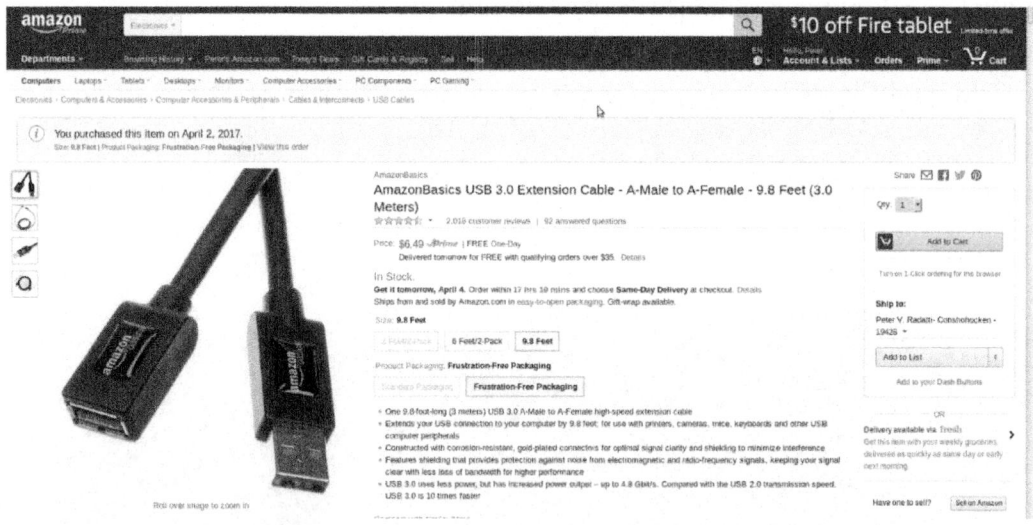

How to Build an Electronic Witness Well for Radionics

Amazon.com 10 Pack CESS Terminal Binding Post Power Audio Amp Plug Banana Jack $6.79

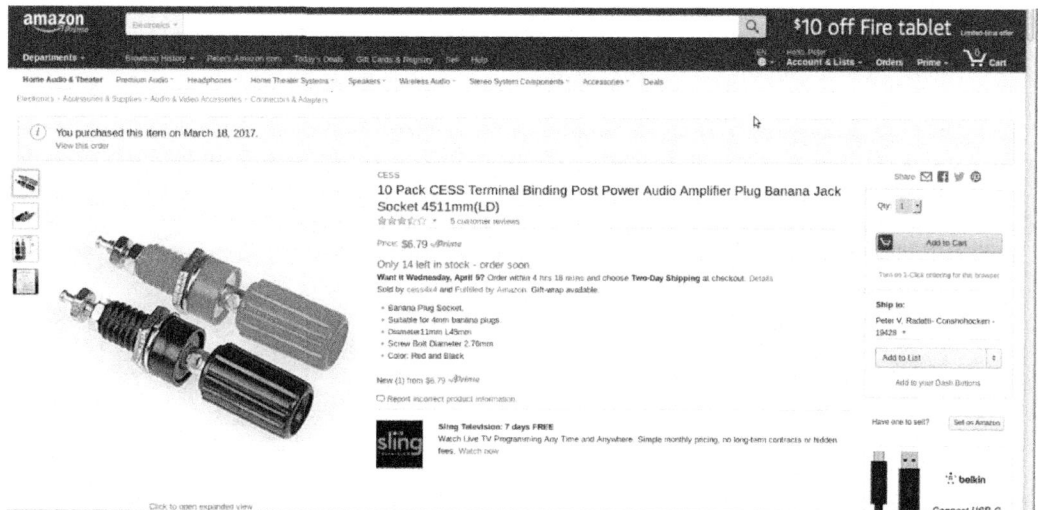

Amazon.com United Scientific WBP024-PK/6 Banana Plug Cord with Two-Way Stackable $14.53

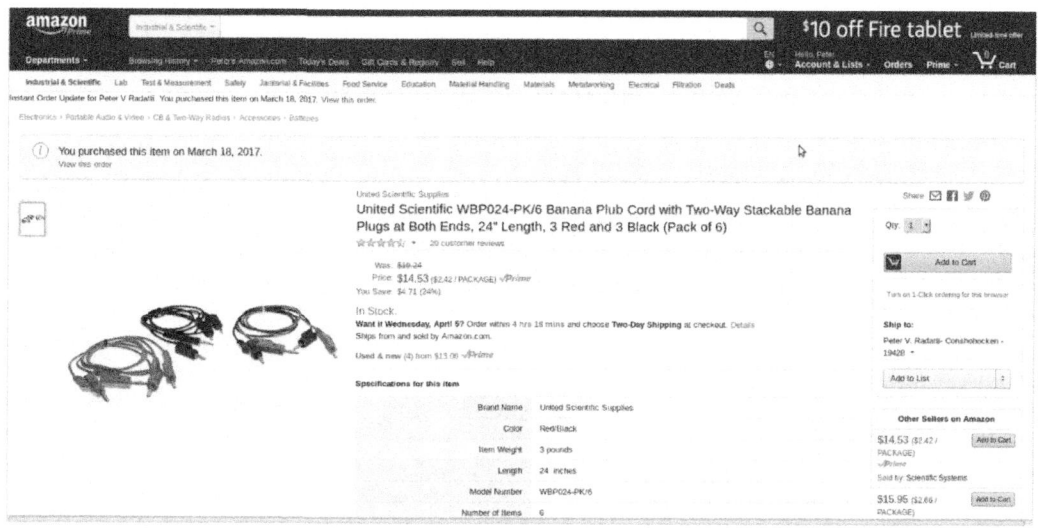

How to Build an Electronic Witness Well for Radionics

Conshohocken Radionics.

If you live near Southeastern Pennsylvania, you might wish to join. Membership and meetings are free. Their website is: http://www.meetup.com/radionics/

Dan Tuck's Manufacturer of Parcel Designed Thea Lamp and other useful devices.
http://www.dtlightworks.com

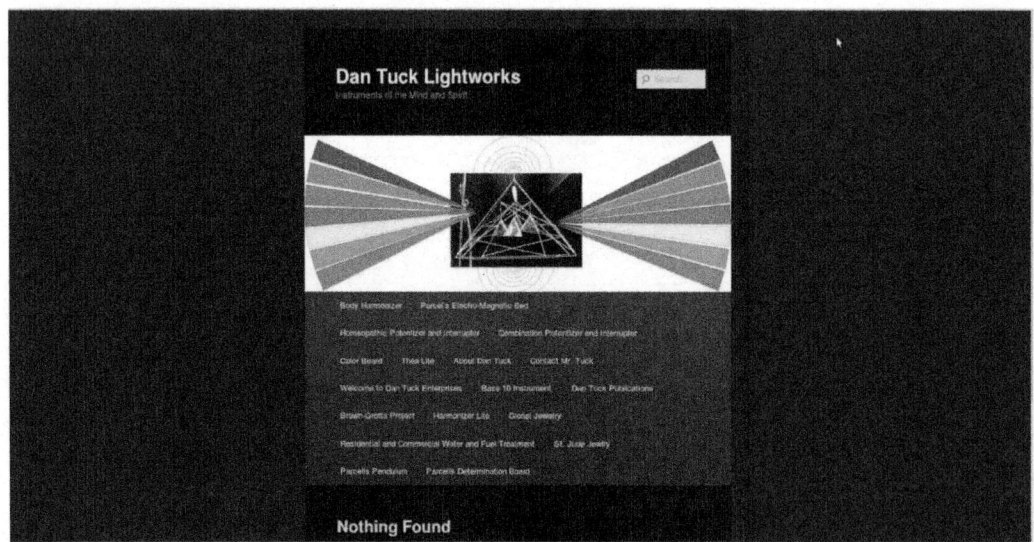

UPDATE: Dan Tuck now sells a version of this Ewell device.

Chapter 9 - Bonus Material

If you want to integrate a computer into the E-Well so you don't have to carry it around or if you want to make your E-Well accessible over the Internet there is a cost effective and simple way of doing this. Use a Raspberry-Pi computer. These are $35 and more powerful than is needed for this project. The only drawback is that you need to know how to configure the system for your purposes. The Raspberry uses Linux as the operating system. See photo below of a Raspberry Pi 2 Model B. (Image courtesy of pixabay.com) This computer contains 4 USB ports, a mini-usb port for power, HDMI and a RJ45 NIC. They can easily be added to a WiFi network.

Radionics Reference Books

The book you are now holding is the third book in the Mastering Radionics Series of books. Here are the first two.

My first book is available in both English and Spanish, low cost digital edition and black and white. A more expensive color version is also available.

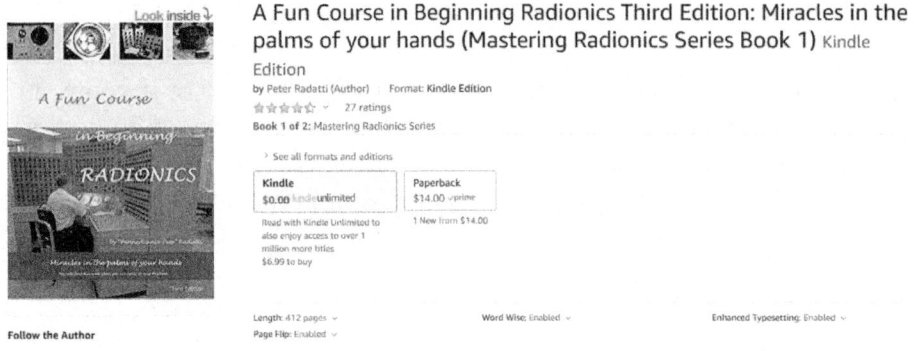

My second book is how to build a special type of electronics well that can hold thousands of witnesses.

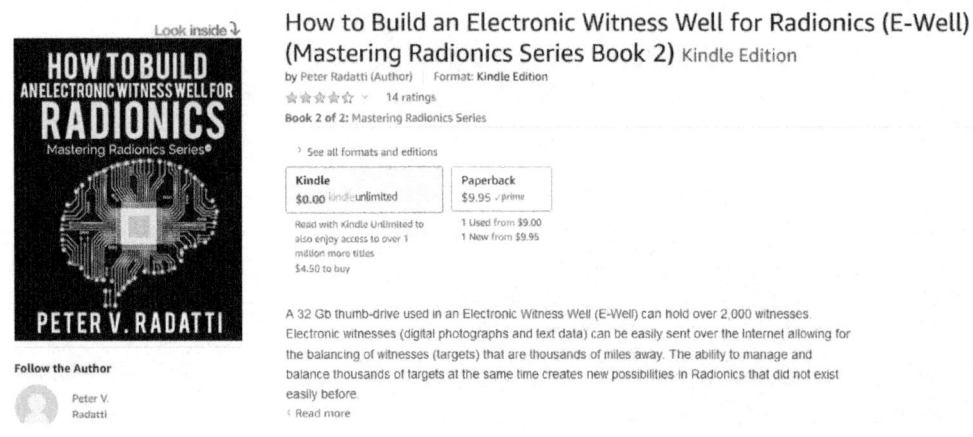

Another book I am suggesting is by a different author. It is a significant work, a multiyear immense work with rates for everything. The important part is that everything is organized for easy location.

How to Build an Electronic Witness Well for Radionics

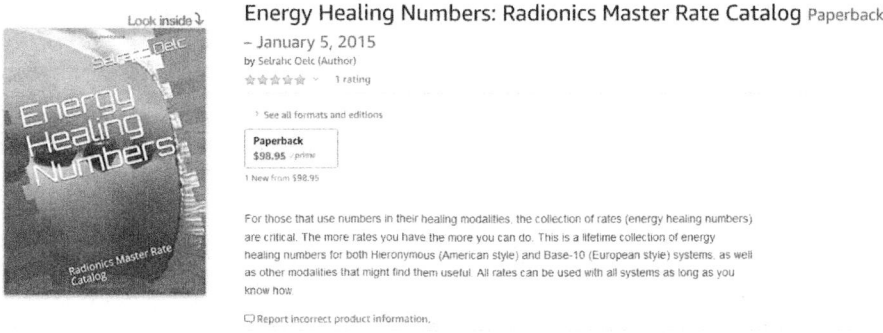

Dan Mangum's book focuses on creating stored rates. "This helpful handbook explains what a reagent is, how they are used in Radionics, and gives the reader creative ideas to apply to their own Radionic work. Many examples of reagents and a wealth of information about them are provided. Symbols, colors, sounds, Sacred Geometry, and more. This book includes a chapter on crafting your own personal reagents. This is the first book in a series of handbooks designed to help educate Radionic practitioners in areas that are not heavily covered in classes or other literature. Applicable to users of Hieronymus, Base 10, Base 44, or other types of Radionic instruments."

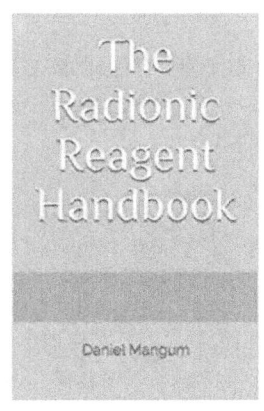

Other Books by Peter V. Radatti

I write books on multiple topics. Here are a few you might be interested in.

This book explains the importance of dietary fiber to the microbiome and your health. The microbiome is critical to your health yet we starve it by not eating the minimum daily requirement of mixed dietary fibers, poison it with preservatives, pesticides, glyphosate and antibiotics contained in our foods.

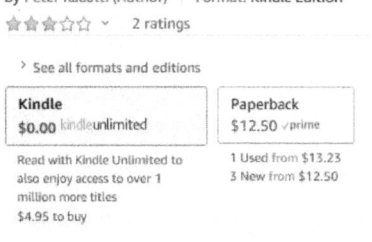

"Microbiome Me" is the second volume of the Dietary Fiber Series by the same author. The first book in the series is: "Dietary Fiber, Essential to the Human Microbiome and Health". ISBN-13: 978-1545015421This book can be read stand-alone but it builds upon the knowledge of the prior book. In this book you will learn about the Gut-Brain-Microbiome connection. How we are killing our

Sciatica and Coccygeal Pain: Sciatica Kindle Edition
by Peter Radatti (Author) Format: Kindle Edition

> See all formats and editions

Kindle	Paperback
$0.00 kindleunlimited	$4.95 ✓prime

Read with Kindle Unlimited to also enjoy access to over 1 million more titles
$2.99 to buy

This book is about a problem that medical science has well in hand but almost no medical doctors know about its treatment. That treatment is called Sacral-Coccyx Adjustment (SCA). The topic is Sciatica and the lower back pain that can radiate down the legs for days, weeks, months and sometimes decades. This pain is often deliberating. The SCA procedure which can be performed in-office to resolve this issue for many people was invented in the year 1623. That is almost 400 years ago. A second newer
‹ Read more

Look inside ↓

Why Would I Want To Be An Ant? Kindle Edition
by Peter Radatti (Author) Format: Kindle Edition

> See all formats and editions

Kindle	Paperback
$0.00 kindleunlimited	$14.50 ✓prime
Read with Kindle Unlimited to also enjoy access to over 1 million more titles	1 New from $14.50
$4.90 to buy	

Large 22 point font, 12 new watercolor panels in full color.
My father told this story to me when I was a child. He explained that his Grandfather told the story to him when he was a child but that the story originally did not contain the ant. My father added the ant. What a critical addition to the story! At some point this story must have been an Italian folktale passed down in our family verbally. I think my father's addition of the ant takes this tale from an interesting story
‹ Read more

Length: 55 pages ⌄   Word Wise: Enabled ⌄   Enhanced Typesetting: Enabled ⌄
Page Flip: Enabled ⌄
Due to its large file size, this book may take longer to download

End of Book
but not of your fun in Radionics!

The Devil gave us Insomnia; God gave us Coffee! - Pete Radatti

Printed in Great Britain
by Amazon